SECRETS OF JAVA

SECRETS OF JAVA

A Self Learning Approach for Students, Academic and Industrial Professionals

By

Er. R. Kabilan, M.E.

Senior Lecturer
Thiruvalluvar College of Engg. and Tech.
Vandavasi (Chennai)

FIREWALL MEDIA

(An Imprint of Laxmi Publications Pvt. Ltd.)

BANGALORE • CHENNAI • COCHIN • GUWAHATI • HYDERABAD
JALANDHAR • KOLKATA • LUCKNOW • MUMBAI • PATNA
RANCHI • NEW DELHI

Published by :
FIREWAL MEDIA
(An Imprint of Laxmi Publications Pvt. Ltd.)
113, Golden House, Daryaganj,
New Delhi-110002

Phone : 011-43 53 25 00
Fax : 011-43 53 25 28

www.laxmipublications.com
info@laxmipublications.com

First Edition : 2009

OFFICES

✆ **Bangalore**	080-26 61 15 61	✆ **Chennai**	044-24 34 47 26
✆ **Cochin**	0484-239 70 04	✆ **Guwahati**	0361-254 36, 69, 251 38 81
✆ **Hyderabad**	040-24 65 23 33	✆ **Jalandhar**	0181-222 12 72
✆ **Kolkata**	033-22 27 43 84	✆ **Lucknow**	0522-220 95 78
✆ **Mumbai**	022-24 91 54 15, 24 92 78 69	✆ **Ranchi**	0651-221 47 64

FSE–3032–085–SECRET OF JAVA

C—

Typeset at : ABRO Enterprises, Delhi.

Printed at : Repro Knowledgecast Limited, Thane

Dedicated to

My Parents,

Brothers & Sisters,

My wife

&

My kids

k. kavini

k. kaviram

and especially to my beloved friends

CONTENTS

PREFACE

Java software is a technology used to develop distributed application executed across all platforms. There are several IDE (Integrated Development Environment) from Sun, Symantec and Borland available in the market. Java uses a compiler to convert the source code into architecture independent byte codes. The JDK (Java Development Kit) from Javasoft contains the basic tools and API (Application Programming Interface) for creating and executing both types of java programs namely application and applet (internet) type programs. This book covers all the important topics of Java programs. Each and every chapter has been prepared with key points and simple examples. I assure that if you read this book you can confidently say that 'I know Java'. This book also contains CD with more examples from all the topics of java, which is pure hard coding that will help you to know the syntax of java very easily.

Every possible attempt has been made to make this book useful for the students, still any suggestions regarding improvement of this book will be acknowledged.

—AUTHOR

ACKNOWLEDGEMENT

My first and foremost thanks to the Almighty for his everlasting love showed upon me throughout this endeavor.

I wish to thank our beloved Chairman/Principal **Dr. S. Arunachalam** and vice principal **Dr. M. Shanmugam**, Thiruvalluvar College of Engg. and Tech., who encouraged and supported me for to bring out this book.

My unbounded thanks to our HOD **Mr. V. Balu, AP** and all my colleagues and friends, who have been inspired to prepare this text.

Last but not the least, my students have given me the thirst and induced me to write this book and I remember them here.

—AUTHOR

Chapter **1**

Introduction

The aim of this book is the user can say that 'I KNOW JAVA', from that the user can develop application and applet (Internet) type programs.

HISTORY OF JAVA

- Java is a pure or true object oriented language developed by sunmicrosystem.
- The first name of java during the year 1991 is oak.
- A team with James gosling developed this language.
- During the year 1995 it is renamed as JAVA.

Why we are choosing this java ?

- Java is a world first platform neutral (independent) language.
- This is the first language supporting and gives the same output with all the operating system.
- From this language we can develop both the application type and internet based applet type programs.

OOPS CONCEPT

There are eight concepts, any language that supports this concept we call that language as object oriented language. They are :

1. **Object** : Instance of class, for example : apple.
2. **Class** : It is a collection of objects of similar type, for example : fruits.
3. **Data abstraction** : The insulation of the data from direct access by the program is called data abstraction or data hiding.
4. **Dynamic binding** : A method call resolved at run time is referred to as dynamic binding.
5. **Data Encapsulation** : The wrapping up of data and method into a single unit is known as data encapsulation.

6. **Inheritance :** Inheritance is the process by which object of one class acquire the properties of another class.
7. **Polymorphism :** A property by which we can send the same message to object of several different classes, that object can respond in a different way depending on its class.
8. **Message passing :** Objects communicate with one another by sending and receiving information.

The language that support program with objects are said to be object based language, for example, javascript

The language that support programming with all the oops concept is known as object-oriented language. For example : c++, JAVA

DEFINITION OF JAVA

JAVA is simple, robust, object oriented, distributed, interpreted, and secures, architecture neutral, portable, high performance, multithreaded, and dynamic language.

Comparison with C

1. Java does not have goto, sizeof and typedef statements.
2. Java does not have data types such as struct, union, and enum.
3. Java does not define modifiers such as auto, extern, register, signed and unsigned,
4. Java does not support preprocessor and pointer.
5. Java adds new operators such as instance of and >>>.

Comparison with C++

1. Java does not support operator overloading except + operator.
2. Java does not directly support multiple inheritance, but this is achieved by interface
3. Java has finalize( ) method corresponding to destructor( ) in c++.
4. Java is an pure object-oriented language.

Software Installation

The software jdk (java development kit) can be downloaded from sun.com or javasoft.com web sites.

This software is compatible with windows'95, windows'98, windows'2000, windows, windows.

After installed the software we get folders like jdk1.1.5, when we move on to jdk1.1.5 folder we get many subfolders from that the important folder is bin within that only all exe files are there.

Commonly we have to set path in autoexec.bat

Path=c:\windows\command;c:\jdk1.5\bin

Path=c:\windows\system32;c:\jdk1.5\bin in windows 'xp

Now we check that the java software is installed or not by type java or javac in dos prompt, if the software is installed that will show like this.

JDK-TOOLS

For java programming we need the following exe files in the bin folder :

1. java.exe – interpreter to run the program
2. javac.exe – java compiler to compile program
3. javap.exe – convert byte code to source code
4. javadoc.exe – to create the documentation
5. javah.exe – source code to byte code
6. jar.exe – to compress the files like win -zip
7. appletviewer.exe – to run applet type program.

Types of Program

By using java we can develop two types' applications :

1. Standalone application type.
2. Internet based applet type.

Steps for executing the standalone application type

1. Create a java program in editor., for example : Dos-prompt edit or Notepad.
2. Save the file with .java extension., for example : Filename.java.
3. Compile the Java Program using javac., for example : javac Filename.java.
4. If there is no error automatically class file will be appear in the directory, for example : Filename.class.
5. To execute the program use the java., for example : java Class name.

Steps for executing the internet based applet type Program

1. Create a java program in editor. For example : Dos-prompt edit or Notepad.
2. Save the file with .java extension., for example : Filename.java.
3. Compile the Java Program using javac., for example : javac Filename.java.
4. If there is no error automatically class file will be appear in the directory, for example : Filename.class.
5. Create a HTML file to call the applet class file by using the following tag for example :<applet code= Classname.class width=200 height=3000></applet>.
6. Save the html file with .htm or .html, for example : Filename.htm.
7. If there is no browser in your system run html file using appletviewer.exe file, for example: appletviewer Filename. java.
8. If browser is there then you can locate the html file and you can see output in browser.

❑❑❑

Chapter **2**

World Wide Web (WWW)

BASICS OF WWW

The CERN (Center European Research Nuclear) developed the technology known as WWW.

Tim Berners – Lee is the author of WWW.

It is developed during year 1989 in Geneva.

The website www.w3c.org gives the information about how the websites should be developed. The w3c is the World Wide Web consortium.

DEFINITION

World Wide Web is the websites contains information about particular organization.

In this portals means the website includes its own information as well as other company information.

URL (Uniform Resource Locator)

It is website address, for example : www.yahoo.com . In which www is the protocol, yahoo is the company name and com represents zones. Generally we call this address is hardware address and it is mapped with software address and loads the web pages of that sites.

For example if www.yahoo.com typed on the address bar of the browser that converts that URL into http ://yahoo.com/index.htm. In which http is a hyper text transport protocol used for navigation of web pages. In which index.htm is the name of source files.

The various zones are :

.com - commercial organization

.edu - educational institution

.net - networking organization

.gov - government sites

.mil - military sites
.org - organization

Some sites URL are with country code for example www.yahoo.co.in.

The various country codes are :

.uk - united kingdom
.in - India
.us - USA
.jp - Japan
.as - Australia

Search Engine

Some sites are having search engine options to find web pages based on the particular topic.

Examples of search engine sites are :

www.google.co.in
www.altavista.com
www.yahoo.co.in
www.infoseek.com

We can classify the entire network into three types, they are :

Intranet

– Means when the same company connected in network for example TCS of different location.

Exteranet

– Means when one company AT different places link with another company. For example : SSi links with TCS for placed the students.

Internet

This is the network of networks, that intranet and extranet links to www internet.

E-mail

E-mail is the one of the service to sending and receiving the messages globally through internet.

There are various free e-mail sites are :

www.hotmail.com
www.yahoo.com
www.lycos.com
www.gmail.com

In that the new user can register the personnel detail and get unique e-mail id. In future you can access this service any where in the world.

You just open e-mail sites enter username and password you can get separate pages in which the message is received and sending the message to others e-mail id.

Many sites provides To, CC, BCC, Subject, Message box. Send, reply, forward and delete options.

We can send message of maximum 50 e-mail id by type the id with comma in To or CC or BCC.

In which cc means carbon copy and bcc means blind carbon copy.

If we send message to one e-mail means you can type the id in TO Textfield or else we can send the same message 25 id means you type that id in cc or bcc with comma.

The difference between CC and BCC is that if we use cc means the receiver can know the others e-mail id also or if we use BCC means the receiver not know the others e-mail id.

❑❑❑

Chapter 3

Hyper Text Markup Language (HTML)

INTRODUCTION

HTML is the very basic fundamental scripting language for developing the web pages. This html is derived from SGML (standard generalized markup language). XML (extensible markup language) also derived from SGML. The only language browser can understand is HTML. During the year 1960 SGML arises as a general purpose scripting language. From that html is derived as scripting language.

HTML TAGS

HTML comprises of tags. Tags means a message with left angle bracket and right angle bracket is known as tags. For example : <html>.

Tags

There are two types' tags :

– opening tag (on code), for example :<html>

– closing tag (off code), for example :</html>

The tag with slash in front of the message is known as closing tag. Some tags have attributes which is used to specify how the web browser should treat a particular tag.

For example :<body bgcolor=red>

HTML file can be developed with notepad or WordPad or front page and save the file with Filename.htm or Filename.html.

No need of any software to installed for HTML. We need editor and browser. The browser contains DTD (Document type definition) which is used to validate the html files.

TYPES OF HTML DTD

(*i*) IEFT level 2 HTML DTD – standard for all browser
(*ii*) IEFT level 3 HTML DTD – under experimental stage
(*iii*) Netscape's Mozilla DTD – developed Netscape Communication Corporation.

BROWSER

It is a software for browse the web pages and to run html files. For example : Internet Explorer from Microsoft, Netscape from Netscape Company, Mozilla firebox and Lynx.

Examples

The entire web pages can be splitted into three parts namely (*i*) Head (*ii*) body (*iii*) footer.

The head tags contain key information about the particular web page. Body part contains all information about that page. And the footer part contain address, e-mail and contact information.

General Structure of HTML File

```
<html>
<head>
<title>TCET</title>
</head>
<body bgcolor=red>
<center> <h1>TCET</h1></center>
<hr>
<marquee>EEE</marquee>
Reaming 80% of tags are included in between the body tag


</body>
</html>
```

It is not a casesentitive; some tags are not having the closing tag. Many of the tags are optional.

Examples of tags : <i>, < b>, <address>, <strong>, <kbd>, <p>, <pre>, <br>, <strike>, <blink>.

❑❑❑

Chapter **4**

Fundamentals of Java

INTRODUCTION

Java is a strictly case sensitive. Java program includes with inbuilt class, methods and variables. The user can also develop class, methods and variables called user defined things.

As per the rules of sunmicrosystem we have to follow certain rules for class name, method name, variables name and object name.

Class Name

Class name first letter is capital. For example : String.

Object Name

Method name first letter is small case and second word first letter is capital, for example : drawLine().

Variables Name

Variables name first letter is any alphabets or underscore or dollar and further we can include the number also.

We should not use the keywords for our own defining purpose.

Program Structure

The general structure of java programming is as follows :

1. Package declaration
2. Import statements
3. Class definitions

Simple example

```
class One
{
    public static void main(String args[])
    {
        System.out.println("Hello World");
    }
}
```

Output

Hello World

In the above program One is user defined class name, public and static is access modifiers, main method is the starting point of application type program, String is built in class name, args[ ] is an user defined array, System is built-in class, out is object, println is method. All the declaration is within the class hence it is called pure object oriented programming.

DATA TYPES

byte	–	8 bits
short	–	16 bits
int	–	32 bits
long	–	64 bits
float	–	32 bits
double	–	64 bits
boolean	–	1 bits
char	–	16 bits

Operators

Arithmetic Operators

Operator	*Meaning*	*Example*
+	Addition	5 + 3
–	Subtraction	5 – 4
*	Multification	10 * 5
/	Division	6 / 3
%	Modulus	5 % 2

```
class Two
{
    public static void main(String args[])
    {
        int x=5, y=5;
        System.out.println("The value of x+y is = " +(x+y));
    }
}
```

Output

The value of x+y is = 10;

Assignment Operators

Expression	*Meaning*
x += y	x = x + y
x –= y	x = x – y
x *= y	x = x * y
x /= y	x = x / y
x = y	x = y

Increment and Decrement Operator

Pre increment operator, for example : ++a

In this case first increment and than assignment

Post increment operator, for example : a++

In this case first assignment and then increment

Pre decrement operator, for example : --a

In this case first decrement and then assignment

Post decrement operator, for example : a—

In this case first assignment and then increment.

Comparison Operators

Operator	*Meaning*
==	Equal
!=	Not equal
<	Less than
>	Greater than
<=	Less than or equal to
>=	Greater than or equal to

Short Circuit Operators && and ||

Why we call this operator as short circuit operator means, if any one side of expression is false means we don't test the other side expression.

Bitwise Operators

&	Bitwise AND
|	Bitwise OR
^	Bitwise XOR
<<	Left shift
>>	Right shift
>>>	Zero fill right shift
~	Bitwise complement

Ternary ? :

SPECIAL OPERATOR

The another two important operator is :

- **dot operator**

  The variables or methods declared with the scope of class are known as instance variable and instance method. To access this variables and methods we can use the below formula

  Syntax : <objectname>.<variablename>

  <objectname>.<methodname>

- **new operator**

  The new operator is used to create the object of a particular class. For example

  Syntax is : Classname objectName = new Classname( );

Keywords

abstract	const	implements	import	package
boolean	false	final	instanceOf	private
break	continue	finally	int	protected
byte	default	float	interface	public
case	do	for	long	return
catch	double	goto	native	transient
char	else	if	short	static
class	extends	new	null	super
synchronized	this	throw	throws	true
try	void	volatile		

Literals

A literal is a value that may be assigned to a primitive or string variable or passed as an argument to a method call.

Example : Boolean isBig = true;

In this true is a literal.

Programming Construct

The construct such as if, for, while, do-while, switch, break, and continue is derived from C programming.

The variables declared within the method are known as local variables. We can directly use the variables name to access its value.

String

String is an inbuilt class of java.lang.String package.

java.lang.* is a default package.

Example :

```
Class strings
{
    int i;
    String names[]={"c++","c","java","oops","oracle"};
    Void show()
    {
        System.out.println("The languages are : ");
        for(i=0;i<names.length();i++)
        {
            System.out.println(names[i]);
        }
    }
    public static void main(String args[])
    {
        strings ss = new strings();
        ss.show();
    }
}
```

Java does not support operator overloading except the + operator.

If any one operand string means the result is concatenation

Example : "10"+10=1010

10+10 = 20;

```
class str
{
    public static void main(String args[])
    {
        String s = "Now is the time for all good men" + "to come to the aid of
                                    their country" + "and pay their taxes";
```

```
        String s1 = "hello world";
        String s2 = "hello";
        String s3 = "HELLO";
        System.out.println(s);
        System.out.println("index of t" +s.idexOf('t'));
        System.out.println("last index of t" +s.lastidexOf('t');
        System.out.println("index of (t, 10)= " +s.idexOf('t',10);
        System.out.println(s1.substring(3,8));
        System.out.println(s2.concat.("world"));
        System.out.println(s2.replace('l','w'));
        System.out.println(s3.toLowerCase());
        System.out.println(s1.trim());
    }
}
```

StringBuffer;

String class static one we cannot change the value and insert and delete at middle of string. But StringBuffer is flexible one we eliminate or insert at middle of the String.

Example :

```
Public class strbuf
{
    public static void main(String args[])
    {
        String too = "too";
        String s = "abc"+too+"def"+Integer.toString(50);
        System.out.println(s);
        StringBuffer sb = new StringBuffer("abc");
        Sb.append(too);
        Sb.append("def");
        Sb.append(Integer.toString(50));
        System.out.println(sb);
    }
}
```

int is the primitive data type, Integer is the wrapper class.

TYPECASTING

Typecasting also possible, *i.e.*, the conversion one data type to another data type.

There are two types type casting namely : 1. Widening 2. Narrowing.

Widening means conversion of small data type to bigger data type.

For example : int to long.

Narrowing means conversion of bigger data type to small data type. In this case loss of data is possible.

For example : long to int.

Syntax : byte s= 10;

int a =(int)s;

In java object type casting also possible.

Arrays

Array is an object used to store the group similar data type elements.

Declarations

int arr[ ];

Creations

int arr[ ] = new int[10];

Initialization

int arr[ ]={1,2,3,4,5};

To find the length of array the formula is arrname.length.

Java supports one dimensional and two dimensional arrays. It does not support multidimensional arrays.

Example :

```
Class array
{
    int I;
    int arr[] = {1,2,3,4,5};
    void disp()
    {
       Sytem.out.println("Display the array list");
       for(int i=0;i<arr.length;i++)
       System.out.println(arr[i]);
    }
    public static void main(String args[])
    {
       array ar = new array();
       ar.disp();
    }
}
```

COMMAND LINE ARGUMENTS

In java the user can fed the input values to the program in two ways 1. command line arguments and Files/streams.

Example :

```
Class carg
{
    public static void main(String args[])
```

```
    {
        System.out.println("The input value is : " +args[0]);
    }
}
compile >javac carg.java
run>java carg "java"
```

Output

The input value is : java

This

This is the keyword. This refers current object.Instead of object name of current class we can use this keyword.

Example :

```
Class point1
{
    int x,y;
    void init(int x, inty)
    {
        this.x=x;
        this.y=y;
    }
    void disp()
    {
        System.out.println(" X- vaue "+x);
    }
    public static void main(String args[])
    {
        point1 pp = new point1();
        pp.init(5,5);
    }
}
```

Constructor

In java constructor name same as class name without return type.

Constructor cannot be overloaded.construtor initializes the object in memory to free of that in c++ destructor is used in java finalize methods are used. And more important point once java program running at background a program or thread run to free of the resources this is called automatic garbage collection.

Access Modifier

public : If we declared class, methods and variables with public modifier any one can access or open to all.

protected : If we declared the variables and methods with protected modifier, it can access in the same class and its subclass.

private : If we declared the variables and methods with private modifier, it can access with in the class only.

static : If we declared the variables and methods with static modifier, it can be accessed by means the class name. For example, Classname.methodname, classname.variablename.

final : If we declared the class, methods and variables with final modifier, final class cannot be make subclasses, final variables cannot change the value. Final methods cannot be overridden by subclass. Local variables cannot be declared as final variables.

Examples of Application Type Program

```
Class sample
{
    public static void main(String args[])
    {
        int x = 10;
        int y = 20;
        float z = 25.2f;
        System.out.println(" The value of x + y is = " +(x + y));
        System.out.println(" The value of x - y is = " +(x - y));
        System.out.println(" The value of x * y is = " +(x * y));
        System.out.println(" The value of x / y is = " +(x / y));
        System.out.println(" The value of z % y is = " +(z % y));
    }
}
```

Comments

// is the single comment

/*multiple line
comment*/

❑❑❑

Chapter **5** # *Inheritance*

INTRODUCTION

Inheritance is the process of deriving features of existing class. The existing class is super class (parent class) where the derived class is subclass (child class). From this the bigger class is subclass because it contains its own features as well as the features of parent class.

In java the top level class (parent class) for all the class is Object class.

The major advantage of inheritance is reusability of existing code.

SINGLE AND MULTIPLE INHERITANCE

When a subclass is derived from a single super class, the inheritance is called single inheritance and when it is derived from more than one super class, it is called as multiple inheritances.

Example :

```
Class woodfurn
{
    String type = "teak";
    String finish = "course";
    Void showdet()
    {
        System.out.println("instance of class " +this.getClass().getName());
        System.out.println("type of wood - " +type);
        System.out.println("finish is - " +finish);
    }
}

class woodtable extends woodfurn
{
    int legs = 5:
```

```
    void show()
    {
        System.out.println("woodtype = "+type);
        System.out.println("finish = "+finish);
        System.out.println("legs = "+legs);
    }
    public static void main(String args[])
    {
        woodtable t = new woodtable();
        t.show();
    }
}
```

Output

woodtype - teak
finish - course
legs - 4

❑❑❑

Chapter **6**

Interface

INTRODUCTION

Java dose not support multiple inheritance directly, but this is achieved by interface. C++ supports multiple inheritances directly. Interface is same class definition but it contains abstract method. Abstract methods means method does not have body and it ends with semicolon.

An interface consists of a set of method definitions. Any class implementing it should provide code for all the methods. Implements are the keyword for using interface. The method should be declared as public and the variables are static and final modifier and it cannot be changed by the class implementing them.

Class a extends b, a is subclass, b is super class

Class a extends b, c is not possible

But

Class a extends b implements c, d - this is possible. c and d are interface.

Class a implements b, b is interface.

Syntax :

```
<acess><interfacename>
{
    <returntype><methodname>(<parameter list>);
    ------
    <type><variablename>=<value>
    -----
}
```

Example :

```
Public interface address
{
    public void add(String add);
    public void name(String name);
}
```

Any class implements this interface has provide code for the methods.

```
Class test implements address
{
    public void add(String a)
    {
        System.out.println("Inside implemented method add()");
        System.out.println("Address :"+a);
    }
    public static void main(String args[])
    {
        test tt = new test();
        tt.add("north road Chennai");
    }
}
```

Output

Address : north road chennai.

❑❑❑

Chapter 7

Packages

INTRODUCTION

Java software contains large number of inbuilt packages.

Example of Inbuilt Package

For example : java.lang.String; java.awt.*; generally we can declare the package as import mainpackage.subpackage.classname;

In this java is main package lang is sub-package and String is inbuilt class.

Each package contains group of large number of related inbuilt class, each class contains inbuilt variables, and methods. We can reuse it for our application.

Package is used to distinguish the same class name.

Implementation of User Defined Package

Steps :

1. Create a directory called pack
2. Open a new file and enter the following code

```
package pack;
public class class1
{
    public static void greet()
    {
        System.out.println("hello");
    }
}
```

3. Save the file as class1.java inside the pack directory.
4. Create a subdirectory called subpack inside the pack directory.

5. Open a file and enter the following code :

```
package pack.subpack;
public class class2
{
    public static void farewell()
    {
        System.out.println("bye");
    }
}
```

6. Save the file as class2.java inside the subpack directory.
7. Open a file in the root directory and enter the following code :

```
import pack.*;
import pack.subpack.*;

class importer
{
    public static void main(String args[])
    {
        class1.greet();
        class2.farewell();
    }
}
```

Output

hello
bye

❑❑❑

Chapter 8 Exceptions

CONCEPT OF EXCEPTIONS

Errors and abnormal conditions arising while executing a program need to be handled.

Exceptions are erroneous events like division by zero, opening a file that does not exist etc.

Exception Key Words

Java handles exceptions using five keywords **try, catch, finally, throws**, and **throw.**

Class Hierarchy

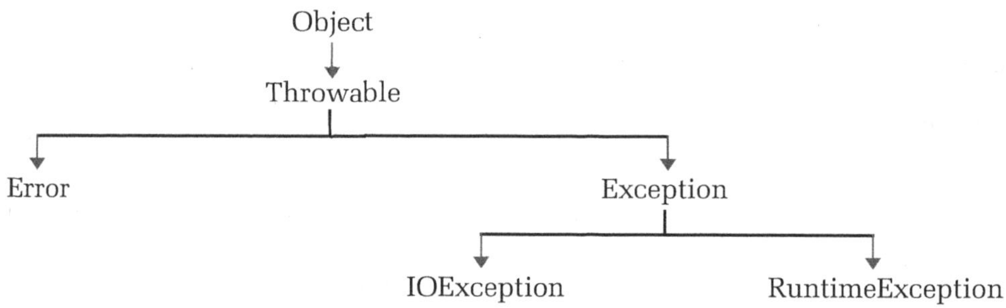

Whenever there is a possibility of an exception being generated in a program, it is better to handle explicitly.

This can be done using the try and catch block. It prevents the program from terminating abruptly.

An error generated code will be placed inside the try block like

Syntax :

```
try
{
    statements;
}
catch(Exception e)
```

```
{
   statements;
}
```

try block should immediately follow one or more catch block or finally block.

If more than one catch block placed means, the first catch should enclosed the super class Exception then the subclass catch block are placed.

Examples for subclass of Exception class

1. ClassNotFoundException
2. IOException
3. SocketException
4. ArithmaticException
5. NumberFormatException
6. ArrayIndexOutofBounceException, etc

If more than one catch block is there means the control search for corresponding matching catch block and executes that catch block, are if there is no corresponding catch block means than it will executes the super class catch block.

```
Class NegTest
{
   public static void main(String args[])
   {
      try
      {
         int arr[] = new int[-2];
         System.out.println("First element :"+arr[0]);
      }
      catch(Exception e)
      {
         System.out.println("super exception");
      }
      catch(NegativeArraySizeException n)
      {
         System.out.println("Sub-class of Exception);
      }

      System.out.println("After the catch block");
   }
}
```

Output

Sub-class of Exception

After the catch block

Finally Block

If we want to execute certain part of code at any cast of moment weather the errors is handles or does not handled, that code is placed in the finally block.

For example if files are opened that should closed, that closing code should be placed in the finally block.

Try block follows either catch block or finally block, if try block follows both catch block and finally block means the finally block should be placed as the last block.

throws

This keyword are used defined along with the method, if we want to throws the exception and not to catch it or handle it means we can use this throws keyword.

```
Class throwsexception
{
    public static void main(String args[])throws ArithmeticException
    {
        System.out.println("inside main");
        int i = 0;
        int j = 40/i
        System.out.println("Iam not coming");
    }
}
```

throw

If we want throw the exception explicitly or if we want create a user defined exception we use the throw keyword.

Syntax :

throw new Exceptionname( );

Example :

```
Class throwdemo
{
    static void demoproc()
    {
        try
        {
            throw new NullPointerException("demo");
        }
        catch(NullPointerException e)
        {
            System.out.println("inside demoproc");
            throw e;
        }
    }
    public static void main(String args[])
    {
        try
        {
            demoproc();
        }
        catch(NullPointerException e)
        {
            System.out.println("recaught : "+e)
        }
    }
}
```

❑❑❑

Chapter 9 IO Streams

DEFINITION

A stream is a sequence of bytes traveling from a source to a destination over a communication path.

If we want to work with input and output files we have import the package java.io.*.

Two Types of Streams

- input streams - for reading purpose
- output streams - for writing purpose

TOP LEVEL CLASSES OF IO PACKAGE

The major top level classes of io package is

– InputStream class

– OutputStream class

– Reader class

– Writer class

– File

– StreamTokenizer

– RandomAccessFile

From this all classes except RandomAcessFile reads and writes the data in sequential manor. The RandomAccessFile reads and write the in non-sequential manner.

The difference between the I/O stream and Reader/Writer class is that the I/O stream read and write in bytes manor, where as the Reader/Writer class are read and write in character manor.

Classes of IO Stream

The pre-defined classes for InputStream and OutputStream are :

InputStream	OutputStream
- SequenceInputStream	- ByteArrayOutputStream
- ByteArrayInputStream	- PipedOutputStream
- FileInputStream	- FileOutputStream
- ObjectInputStream	- FilterOutPutStream
- PipedInputStream	- BufferedOutputStream
- FilterInputStream	- DataOutputStream
- PushBackInputStream	- ObjectOutputStream
- BufferedInputStream	
- DataInputStream	

Sub-Classes of Reader/Writer classes

The pre-defined classes for Reader and Writer are :

Reader	Writer
- BufferedReader	- BufferedWriter
- CharArrayReader	- CharArrayWriter
- StringReader	- Filterwriter
- PipedReader	- StringWriter
- InputStreamReader	- PipedWriter
- FilterReader	- PrintWriter
- OutputStreamWriter	

DataI/OStream - used for reading and writing of primitive data types

PipedI/Ostream - used for the transfer of data between threads

ObjectI/OStream- used for read and writer the object to the stream

Example of Methods

The important methods of InputStream/Reader classes are :

- read( ) - read bytes from input source
- skip( ) - skip the bytes of input
- available( ) - bytes currently available for reading
- close ( ) - close the input source
- mark( ) - marks current point in stream
- reset - returns input pointer to previously set mark

The important methods of OuputStream/Writer classes are :

- write( ) - writes the data to output
- flush( ) - finalizes output state to clear the buffer
- close( ) - closes output stream

Examples :

```
import java.io.*;

class FileMethod1
{
   public static void main(String args[])
   {
      File f1 = new File("kabilan","hello.txt");
      //File f2 = new File(f1.getParent());

      System.out.println("parent: " + f1.getParent());
      System.out.println("File name: " + f1.getName());
      System.out.println("Path: " + f1.getPath());
      System.out.println("Absolute: " + f1.getAbsolutePath());
      System.out.println(f1.exists()?"file exists":"file does not exists");
      System.out.println(f1.isDirectory()?"f1 is a directory":"f1 is not directory");
      System.out.println(f1.isFile()?"file exists":"file does not exists");
      //System.out.println("parent:f2 " + f2.getParent());

   }
}


//pgm to test the rename and delete method
import java.io.*;

class FileMethod2
{
   public static void main(String args[])
   {
      for(int i=0;i<args.length;i++)
      {
         File f1 = new File("i:/kabilan/newr",args[i]);
         File f2 = new File("i:/kabilan/newr/kill.txt");
         if(f1.exists())
         {
            System.out.println(f1 + "does exists.");
            System.out.println("size is" + f1.length() + "bytes");
            f1.renameTo(f2);
         }
         else
         System.out.println(f1 +"does not exists");
      }
   }
}
```

```
import java.io.*;

public class FileMethod3 implements FilenameFilter
{
   String z;

   public FileMethod3(String w)
   {
      this.z="." + w;
   }
   public boolean accept(File dir,String name)
   {
      return name.endsWith(z);
   }
   public static void main(String args[]) throws IOException
   {
      for(int p = 0;p<args.length;p++)
      {
         File f1 = new File("i:/kabilan/newr/inou");
         FilenameFilter only = new FileMethod3(args[p]);
         String s[] = f1.list(only);

         for(int i = 0;i<s.length;i++)
         {
            System.out.println(s[i]);
         }
      }
   }
}
```

```
import java.io.*;
public class Linr
{
   public static void main(String args[])throws Exception
   {
      FileReader fr = new FileReader("Linr.java");

      LineNumberReader lnr = new LineNumberReader(fr);
      String str;
      while((str=lnr.readLine())!=null)
      {
         System.out.println(lnr.getLineNumber()+"."+str);
      }
   }
}
```

```
import java.io.*;

public class Ran
{
   public static void main(String args[])throws Exception
   {
      RandomAccessFile ra = new RandomAccessFile("kill.txt","rw");
      //RandomAcessFile ra = new RandomAccessFile("kill.txt",r);

      ra.writeInt(1234);
      ra.writeDouble(12.5);
      ra.writeBoolean(true);
      ra.seek(0);
      System.out.println(ra.readInt());
      long pp = ra.getFilePointer();
      System.out.println(pp);
      ra.seek(pp);
      System.out.println(ra.readDouble());
      ra.seek(2);
      System.out.println(ra.readBoolean());
      System.out.println(ra.length());
   }
}
```

```
import java.io.*;

public class Word
{
   public static void main(String args[])throws IOException
   {
      FileReader fr = new FileReader("i:/kabilan/newr/inou/aa.txt");
      StreamTokenizer input = new StreamTokenizer(fr);
      int tok;
      int count = 0;

      while((tok = input.nextToken()) != StreamTokenizer.TT_EOF)
      if(tok == StreamTokenizer.TT_WORD)
      {
         //System.out.println("Word Found: "+ input.nval);
         System.out.println("Word Found: "+ input.sval);
         count++;
      }
      System.out.println("Found "+count+"words in aa.txt");
   }
}
```

```
import java.io.*;

class DataStream
{
    public static void main(String args[])throws IOException
    {
        BufferedReader d = new BufferedReader(new
        InputStreamReader(new FileInputStream("i:/kabilan/newr/inou/aa.txt")));
        DataOutputStream o = new DataOutputStream(new
        FileOutputStream("i:/kabilan/newr/inou/temp1.txt"));

        String line;
        while((line = d.readLine())!=null)
        {
            String a = (line.toUpperCase());
            System.out.println(a);
            o.writeBytes(a+ "\r\n");
        }
        d.close();
        o.close();
    }
}
```

❑❑❑

Chapter 10 AWT

INTRODUCTION

The Abstract Windowing Toolkit (AWT) is an API that is responsible for building the Graphical User Interface (GUI). It is a part of the Java Foundation Classes (JFC). AWT includes a rich set of user interface components, a powerful event handling model, graphics and image tools, layout managers and support for data transfer using cut and paste through clipboards. AWT also supports JavaBeans architecture. Every AWT component is a simple bean. The java.awt.* package contains all classes for creating user interface and for painting graphics and images.

AWT package contains *n* number of class. Examples Graphics, Color, Font. Each class contains *n* number of constructor, methods and variables.

If we want know the methods and variables of particular class we can use the following syntax

>javap java.awt.Graphics > a.txt

The details of this particular class are stored in a.txt file, open that text file and see the details.

If we want to create the help or documentation of the particular user defined java program means use the following syntax

>javadoc Filename.java

It will give output in html file.

One more important point is the top level or super class of all java class is **Object.**

LAYOUT MANAGERS

The java.awt.LayoutManager helps to position the components in a container.

The basic Layout Managers are

1. FlowLayout - Left to Right arrangement of components
2. BorderLayout - Arrange components in North, South, East, West and center

3. GridLayout - Arrange components in row and column wise
4. GridBagLayout - This is the Layout arrange components as per the User requirements
5. CardLayout - This Layout is used to arrange the components one on top of another

The Examples for components are :

1. Button
2. TextField
3. TextArea
4. Checkbox
5. Label
6. Choice
7. List
8. Scrollbar

The Examples for Container is

1. Panel
2. Frame
3. Applet

EVENT HANDLERS

ActionListener, MouseListener, FocusListeners, WindowListeners, etc, all this Listeners with abstract methods, the class implements this Listeners should provide the body of that method.

Examples :

```
import java.awt.*;
import java.applet.*;
import java.awt.event.*;
class frame extends Frame
{
    boolean a;
    frame()
    {
        a=false;
        addWindowListener(new W());
    }
    class w extends WindowClosing(WindowEvent e)
    {
        dispose();
        System.exit(0);
    }
}
public class frame extends Applet
{
```

```
    int num = 0;
    public void init()
    {
       Button b= new Button("create window");
       b.addActionListener(new B());
       add(b);
    }
    class B implements ActionListener
    {
       public void actionPerformed(ActionEvent e)
       {
          frame mf = new frame();
          mf.setVisible(true);
          mf.setSize(300,300);
          mf.setTitle("Amjath:" +num);
          ++num;
       }
    }
}
```

```
import java.awt.*;
import java.applet.*;
import java.awt.event.*;

public class FlowL extends Frame
{
    Panel p1,p2,p3,p4;
    String str[]={"one","two","three","four","five","seven"};
    FileDialog ff;
    FlowL()
    {
       addWindowListener(new winclo());
       setTitle("Layout");
       setLayout(new BorderLayout());
       p1 = new Panel();
       p2 = new Panel();
       p3 = new Panel();
       p4 = new Panel();
       ff = new FileDialog(this,"save",FileDialog.SAVE);
       TextField tf1 = new TextField(30);
       TextField tf2 = new TextField(30);
       TextField tf3 = new TextField(30);
       TextArea ta = new TextArea();
       p1.setBackground(Color.gray);
```

```
        p2.setBackground(Color.black);
        p1.setLayout(new GridLayout(2,3,10,10));
        p2.setLayout(new BorderLayout());
        p3.setBackground(Color.yellow);
        p3.setLayout(new FlowLayout(FlowLayout.LEFT));
        p3.setBackground(Color.blue);
        p4.setLayout(new GridBagLayout());
        for(int i=0;i<str.length;i++)
        {
           p1.add(new Button(str[i]));
        }
        p2.add("North",new Button("N"));
        p2.add("South",new Button("s"));
        p2.add("East",new Button("e"));
        p2.add("West",new Button("w"));
        p2.add("Center",new Button("c"));

        p3.add(new Button("b1gghgggg"));
        p3.add(new Button("b2"));
        p3.add(new Button("b3"));
        p3.add(new Button("b4"));

        p4.add(tf1);
        p4.add(tf2);
        p4.add(tf3);


        add(ta,BorderLayout.CENTER);
        add(p1,BorderLayout.EAST);
        add(p2,BorderLayout.WEST);
        add(p3,BorderLayout.SOUTH);
        add(p4,BorderLayout.NORTH);

     }
     public static void main(String args[])
     {
        FlowL ff = new FlowL();
        ff.setSize(300,300);
        ff.setVisible(true);
     }
     class winclo extends WindowAdapter
     {
        public void windowClosing(WindowEvent e)
        {
           //dispose();
```

```
        ff.show();
      }
    }
}


import java.awt.*;
import java.applet.*;

/*<applet code = "color.java" width=300 height=200>
</applet>*/

public class color extends Applet
{
    public void init()
    {
       setBackground(Color.blue);
       setForeground(Color.yellow);
    }

    public void paint(Graphics g)
    {
       Font f = new Font("Times Roman",Font.BOLD,20);

       Font f1= new Font("Courier",Font.PLAIN,20);
       Font f2 = new Font("helvetica",Font.ITALIC,20);
       Color rr = new Color(255,175,175);
       g.setColor(Color.blue);
       g.setFont(f);
       g.drawString("be happy,be hopefull",30,30);
       g.setColor(Color.yellow);
       g.setFont(f1);
       g.drawString("be happy, be hopefull",30,60);
       g.setColor(rr);
       g.setFont(f2);
       g.drawString("be happy, be hopefull",30, 110);
    }
}

import java.awt.event.*;
import java.awt.*;
public class action extends Frame implements
ActionListener,FocusListener//,MouseListener,MouseMotionListener//,KeyListener,
{
    Button btn;
```

```
TextField tf1,tf2,tf3;
TextArea ta;
Panel pn;
public action()
{
   btn = new Button("click me");
   tf1 = new TextField(30);
   tf2 = new TextField(30);
   tf3 =new TextField(30);
   ta = new TextArea(30,30);
   pn = new Panel();

   pn.setLayout(new FlowLayout());
   pn.add(btn);
   pn.add(tf1);
   pn.add(tf2);
   pn.add(ta);
   pn.add(tf3);
   add(pn);
   btn.addActionListener(this);
   addWindowListener(new win());
   tf2.addKeyListener(new kk());
   ta.addMouseListener(new mn());
   ta.addMouseMotionListener(new mm());
   tf3.addFocusListener(this);
}
// class bb extends Button implements ActionListener
// {
      public void actionPerformed(ActionEvent e)
      {
         if(e.getSource()==btn)
         tf1.setText("ok");
      }
// }
class win extends WindowAdapter// implements WindowListener
{
   public void windowClosing(WindowEvent e)
   {
      System.exit(0);
   }
}
class kk extends KeyAdapter
{
   public void keyPressed(KeyEvent e)
   {
```

```
        // System.out.println("aciotnm");
        tf2.setText("String()");
    }
}
class mn extends MouseAdapter
{
    public void mouseReleased(MouseEvent e)
    {
        ta.setText("out");
    }
}
class mm extends MouseMotionAdapter
{
    public void mouseMoved(MouseEvent e)
    {
        ta.setText("in");
    }
}
public void focusLost(FocusEvent e)
{
    tf3.setText("lost");
}
public void focusGained(FocusEvent e)
{
    tf3.setText("Gain");
}
public static void main(String args[])
{
    action aa = new action();
    aa.setSize(300,200);
    aa.setVisible(true);
    }
}
```

```
import java.awt.*;
import java.awt.event.*;

public class bar extends Frame implements ActionListener
{
    Label l1,l2,l3,l4;
    TextField t1,t2,t3,t4;
    Button b1,b2,b3;
    Choice c1,c2;
    Panel p1,p2,p3;
```

```
bar()
{
   setTitle("Medical");
   p1 = new Panel();
   p1.setLayout(new GridLayout(4,2));

   l1 = new Label("asd");
   l2 = new Label("asd");
   l3 = new Label("ad");
   l4 = new Label("asd");

   t1 = new TextField(10);
   t2 = new TextField(10);
   t3 = new TextField(10);
   t4 = new TextField(10);

   p2 = new Panel();
   p2.setLayout(new FlowLayout());

   b1 = new Button("add");
   b2 = new Button("Dee");
   b3 = new Button("ok");

   p3 = new Panel();
   p3.setLayout(new FlowLayout());

   c1 = new Choice();
   c1.add("sds");
   c1.add("df");

   p1.add(l1);
   p1.add(t1);
   p1.add(l2);
   p1.add(t2);
   p1.add(l3);
   p1.add(t3);
   p1.add(l4);
   p1.add(t4);
   p2.add(b1);
   p2.add(b2);
   p2.add(b3);
   p3.add(c1);

   this.setLayout(new GridLayout(3,1));
   this.add(p1);
```

```
        this.add(p2);
        this.add(p3);
        b1.addActionListener(this);
    }
    public static void main(String args[])
    {
        bar bb = new bar();
        bb.setSize(300,300);
        bb.setVisible(true);
    }
    public void actionPerformed(ActionEvent e)
    {
        if(e.getSource()==b1)
        System.exit(0);
    }
}
```

```
import java.awt.*;
import java.awt.event.*;

class MyAppl extends Frame implements ActionListener
{
    MenuBar Mb;
    Menu M;
    MenuItem mi1, mi2;
    public MyAppl()
    {
        Mb = new MenuBar();
        M = new Menu("Menu");
        mi1 = new MenuItem("Item 1");
        mi2 = new MenuItem("Item 2");
        M.add(mi1);
        M.add(mi2);
        Mb.add(M);
        setMenuBar(Mb);
        setTitle("Sample Stand alone Application");
        mi1.addActionListener(this);
        mi2.addActionListener(this);
    }
    public static void main(String a[])
    {
        MyAppl m = new MyAppl();
        m.setVisible(true);
        m.setSize(300,400);
    }
```

```
    public void actionPerformed(ActionEvent ae)
    {
        MenuItem m = (MenuItem) ae.getSource ();
        if(m == mi1)
        setTitle("Menu Item 1 Selected");
        if(m == mi2)
        setTitle("Menu Item 2 Selected");
    }
}
```

```
import java.awt.*;
import java.awt.event.*;

class dialog extends Dialog
{
    public dialog(Frame F, String s)
    {
        super(F, s);
        Label l = new Label("User Defined Dialog Box");
        setSize(200,200);
        add(l);
    }
}
class Dial extends Frame implements ActionListener
{
    MenuBar Mb;
    Menu M;
    MenuItem Mi1, Mi2;
    public Dial()
    {
        Mb = new MenuBar();
        M = new Menu("Menu");
        Mi1 = new MenuItem("Dialog");
        Mi2 = new MenuItem("File Dialog");
        M.add(Mi1);
        M.add(Mi2);
        Mb.add(M);
        Mi1.addActionListener(this);
        Mi2.addActionListener(this);
        setMenuBar(Mb);
    }
    public static void main(String a[])
    {
        Dial D = new Dial();
```

```
        D.setVisible(true);
        D.setSize(400,500);
      }
    public void actionPerformed(ActionEvent ae)
    {
        String df = new String();
        MenuItem Mf = (MenuItem)ae.getSource();
        if(Mf == Mi1)
        {
            dialog d = new dialog(this, "Dialog Demo");
            d.setVisible(true);
        }
        if(Mf == Mi2)
        {
            FileDialog Fd = new FileDialog(this, "File");
            Fd.show();
            if(Fd.getFile()!=null)
            {
                df = Fd.getFile();
                df += Fd.getDirectory();
                setTitle(df);
            }
        }
    }
}
```

❑❑❑

Chapter **11** ***Applet***

INTRODUCTION

An applet is a dynamic and interactive program that can run inside a Web page displayed by a Java-capable browser such as Hot Java, Lynx, Netscape or Internet Explorer. Hot Java Browser is a World Wide Web browser used to view web pages, follow links and submit forms. It can also downloaded and play applets on our system.

Simply we call applet program is an internet program view on web pages. This is another type of java program. If there is no browser in our system means we can use tools appletviewer.exe to execute applet program. This applet window is just embedded in the browser. We can see the status bar of browser applet started is displayed from that we can identify that web page contains applet program. If we want execute the applet in browser means we need to develop html file and call the applet class file in html file and locate the html file in browser. For developing applet program we have import java.applet.* package. The minimum requirements of html tags for applet is given below.

HTML Tag Requirements for Applet

<applet code=Appletclassfilename.class width = 300 height=300></applet>

Restrictions of Applet

1. Applets cannot read or write to the file system.
2. Applets cannot communicate with any other server.
3. Applet cannot run any programs on the System.

LIFE CYCLE OF APPLET

1. **init( )** : This method gets called as soon an applet is started. Initialization of all variables are done here.
2. **start( )** : This method is executed after the init () method. The stage is currently we viewing the web page.
3. **stop( )** : If we are moving other than applet page that time stop () method is called, and if we come to the applet again start () method is called.
4. **destroy( )** : When we are closing the web pages that time destroy () method is called.

Examples :

```
import java.applet.*;
import java.awt.*;

public class FirstApplet extends Applet
{
    public void paint(Graphics g)
    {
        g,drawstring("Hello World",50,50);
    }
}
```

If the package contains * means it will search and import the required class. Anyway it is safer means it will take more time when compared to this java.applet.Applet syntax.

Graphics are class of AWT package

drawString ("String", x-coordinates, y-coordinates) is method of graphics class.

The html file contains the following tag for executing the above applet program.

```
<applet code=FirstApplet.class width =300 height=400></applet>

import java.awt.*;
import java.applet.*;

public class ParamTest extends Applet
{
    Font ff = new Font("TimesRoman", Font.BOLD, 35);
    String name;
    Public void init()
    {
        name = getParameter("name");
        if(name == null)
            name = "Friend";
            name = "Have a good day" + name;
    }
    public void paint(Graphics g)
    {
        g.setFont(ff);
        g.setColor(Color.red);
        g.drawString(name, 50, 50);
    }
}
```

The html files is

```
<applet code = ParamTest.class width=300 height=400>
<param Name = name value = "APPLET">
```

```
</aaplet>

import java.awt.*;
import java.applet.*;
import java.awt.event.*;
import javax.swing.*;

public class awt extends Frame implements ActionListener
{
   Button btn1,btn2;
   Label l1;
   Checkbox cb1,cb2;
   Choice cc;
   CheckboxGroup cbg;
   JFileChooser fd;

   awt()
   {
      setLayout(new GridLayout(3,3));
      btn1 = new Button("ok");
      btn2 = new Button("cancel");
      l1 = new Label("clickme");
      cbg = new CheckboxGroup();
      cb1 = new Checkbox("male",cbg,true);
      cb2 = new Checkbox("fma",cbg,false);
      fd = new JFileChooser("s:/kabilan/");

      cc = new Choice();
      cc.add("dfdf");
      cc.add("dfdf");
      cc.add("dfdf");
      btn1.addActionListener(this);
      btn2.addActionListener(this);
      add(btn1);
      add(btn2);
      add(l1);
      add(cb1);
      add(cb2);
      add(cc);
   }
   public void actionPerformed(ActionEvent e)
   {
      if(e.getSource()==btn1)
      {
         System.out.println("the hashcode"+ btn1.hashCode());
         System.out.println("sdfd");
         fd.show();
      }
   }
```

```
    public static void main(String args[])
    {
        awt aa = new awt();
        aa.setSize(300,300);
        aa.setVisible(true);
    }
}
```

```
import java.awt.*;
import java.awt.event.*;
import java.applet.*;
/*
<applet code="But.class" height=400 width=400>
</applet>
*/
public class But extends Applet implements ActionListener, MouseListener
{
    Button b1, b2;
    TextField Tf;
    List L1;
    String d;
    Checkbox c1, c2;
    public void init ()
    {
        b1 = new Button("Add");
        b2 = new Button("Select");
        L1 = new List(5, true);
        Tf = new TextField("Hello", 10);
        c1 = new Checkbox("Male",false, new CheckboxGroup ());
        c2 = new Checkbox("Female",true, new CheckboxGroup ());
        add(b1);
        add(L1);
        add(Tf);
        add(b2);
        add(c1);
        add(c2);
        b1.addActionListener(this);
        b2.addActionListener(this);
        c1.addMouseListener(this);
        c2.addMouseListener(this);
    }
    public void paint(Graphics g)
    {
        g.drawString("Controls Demo", 40,50);
    }
    public void actionPerformed(ActionEvent ae)
    {
        Button b = (Button) ae.getSource();
```

```
        String s = b.getLabel();
        String d = new String();
        if(s.equals("Add"))
        L1.add(Tf.getText ());
        else if(s.equals ("Select"))
        {
            String a[] = L1.getSelectedItems();
            for(int i=0; i<a.length; i++)
            d+= a[i];
            showStatus(d);
        }
    }
    public void mouseClicked(MouseEvent ae)
    {
        Checkbox v = (Checkbox) ae.getSource();
        String s = v.getLabel();
        if(v==c1)
        {
            showStatus("Male Selected...");
            c1.setState(true);
            c2.setState(false);
        }
        else if(v==c2)
        {
            showStatus("Female Selected...");
            c1.setState(false);
            c2.setState(true);
        }
    }
    public void mouseEntered(MouseEvent me) {}
    public void mouseExited(MouseEvent me){}
    public void mousePressed(MouseEvent me) {}
    public void mouseReleased(MouseEvent me) {}

}
```

```
import java.applet.*;
import java.awt.*;

//<applet code=Grid width=300 height=200></applet>

public class Grid extends Applet
{
    TextArea ta;
    TextField tf;
    Button b1,b2,b3;
    Choice ch;
    GridBagLayout gbl;
```

```
GridBagConstraints gbc;

public void init()
{
   gbl = new GridBagLayout();
   setLayout(gbl);
   gbc = new GridBagConstraints();
   ta = new TextArea("Java",10,10);
   tf = new TextField(10);
   ch = new Choice();
   ch.addItem("one");
   ch.addItem("two");
   ch.addItem("three");
   b1 = new Button("one");
   b2 = new Button("two");
   b3 = new Button("three");

   gbc.fill = GridBagConstraints.BOTH;
   addCom(ta,gbl,gbc,0,0,1,3);

   gbc.fill = GridBagConstraints.HORIZONTAL;
   addCom(b1,gbl,gbc,0,1,2,1);

   gbc.weightx=1;
   gbc.weighty=1;
   gbc.fill = GridBagConstraints.BOTH;
   addCom(b2,gbl,gbc,1,1,1,1);

   gbc.weightx=0;
   gbc.weighty=0;
   addCom(b3,gbl,gbc,3,0,2,1);
   addCom(tf,gbl,gbc,1,2,1,1);
   addCom(ch,gbl,gbc,2,2,1,1);
}
public void addCom(Component c, GridBagLayout g, GridBagConstraints gc,
                        int row, int column, int width, int height)
{
   gc.gridx=column;
   gc.gridy=row;
   gc.gridwidth=width;
   gc.gridheight=height;
   g.setConstraints(c,gc);
   add(c);
}
}
```

❑❑❑

Chapter 12 Swings

INTRODUCTION

JDK1.2 was introduced with a new set of packages the java Foundation classes (JFC) that includes an improved user interface components called swing components.

JFC or swing is an extension of AWT not a replacement of AWT. The classes of AWT are valid for swing components.

COMPARISON WITH AWT

Awt components application has given different look and feel in different, different platforms. This is one of the disadvantages of AWT Components. Sun-Microsystems developed a new version JFC1.2 or Swing components to give same look and feel application in all platforms.

JFC1.2 consists of five major package :

1. Swing
2. Pluggable Look and Feel
3. Drag and Drop
4. Accessibility
5. 2D.

The swing components facilitate efficient graphical user interface (GUI) development. These components are a collection of lightweight visual components. The root class of all swing components is JComponent which is derived from Container of AWT package so that only we call swing is an extension of AWT not an replacement of AWT.

Syntax

The programming way is some what different when compared to AWT. In swing components all the class names are start with capital J.

For example AWT Class is Button.

For example swing class is JButton. This is the only difference in syntax wise. So swing is an improved version of AWT and it has some additional components also.

Examples :

```
import java.awt.*;
import javax.swing.*;
import java.awt.event.*;
import javax.swing.border.*;

/*<applet code=card width=300 height=200>
</applet>*/

public class card extends JApplet implements ActionListener
{
    JPanel p1,p2;
    CardLayout c1;
    public void init()
    {

        p1 = new JPanel();
        p2 = new JPanel();

        p2.setLayout(new FlowLayout());
        p2.setBackground(Color.orange);


        JButton btn1 = new JButton("Firsthjghgjhg");
        JButton btn2 = new JButton("Secondkjhlkhkl");
        JButton btn3 = new JButton("Thirdioyihh");

        JButton btn4 = new JButton("Action");

        c1 = new CardLayout();

        p1.setLayout(c1);
        p1.add("First",btn1);
        p1.add("Second",btn2);
        p1.add("Third",btn3);

        this.getContentPane().add(p2);

        p2.add(p1);
        p2.add(btn4);
        btn4.addActionListener(this);

        Border line = BorderFactory.createLineBorder(Color.black,5);
        btn1.setBorder(line);
        btn2.setBorder(BorderFactory.createLineBorder(Color.red,5));
```

```
        btn3.setBorder(BorderFactory.createLineBorder(Color.green,5));
        p1.setBorder(new BevelBorder(BevelBorder.RAISED));
        p2.setBorder(new BevelBorder(BevelBorder.RAISED));
        // p2.setBorder(BorderFactory.createLineBorder(Color.black,5));
    }
    public void actionPerformed(ActionEvent ae)
    {
        c1.next(p1);
    }
}
```

```
import javax.swing.*;
import java.awt.*;
import javax.swing.border.*;

/*<applet code = japp width=300 height=200>
</applet>*/

public class japp extends JApplet
{
    String ct[]={"India","usa","japan","canada"};
    public void init()
    {
        getContentPane().setLayout(new FlowLayout());

        JButton btn = new JButton("Click",new ImageIcon("Paris.gif"));;
        btn.setMnemonic('l');
        JCheckBox jb = new JCheckBox("select");
        JLabel jbl = new JLabel("Name");
        JTextField jtf = new JTextField(30);
        JTextArea jta = new JTextArea(10,10);
        JList jls = new JList(ct);
        JComboBox jcb = new JComboBox();
        jcb.addItem("aaa");
        jcb.addItem("bbb");
        jcb.addItem("ccc");
        jcb.addItem("ddd");

        JScrollPane jsc1 = new
        JScrollPane(jls,JScrollPane.VERTICAL_SCROLLBAR_ALWAYS,JScrollPane.
        HORIZONTAL_SCROLLBAR_AS_NEEDED);
        JScrollPane jsc2 = new
        JScrollPane(jta,JScrollPane.VERTICAL_SCROLLBAR_ALWAYS,JScrollPane.
        HORIZONTAL_SCROLLBAR_AS_NEEDED);
```

```
        getContentPane().add(jcb);
        getContentPane().add(jsc1);
        getContentPane().add(jsc2);
        getContentPane().add(jbl);
        getContentPane().add(jtf);
        getContentPane().add(btn);
        getContentPane().add(jb);

        Border line =BorderFactory.createLineBorder(Color.red,5);
        btn.setBorder(line);
        Border line1 =BorderFactory.createLineBorder(Color.yellow,5);
        jta.setBorder(line1);
    }
}
```

```
import javax.swing.*;
import java.awt.*;
//<applet code = BoxDemo width=300 height=200></applet>
public class BoxDemo extends JApplet
{
    public void init()
    {

        Box bb = new Box(BoxLayout.Y_AXIS);

        JButton btn1 = new JButton("one");
        JButton btn2 = new JButton("two");
        JButton btn3 = new JButton("three");
        bb.add(btn1);
        bb.add(btn2);
        bb.add(btn3);
        getContentPane().add(bb);
    }
}
```

```
import java.awt.*;
import javax.swing.*;
/*
<applet code="JLabelDemo" width=300 height=200>
</applet>
*/

public class JLabelDemo extends JApplet {
```

```
        public void init() {

        Container contentPane = getContentPane();

        ImageIcon ii = new ImageIcon("france.gif");

        JLabel j1 = new JLabel("France", ii, JLabel.CENTER);

        contentPane.add(j1);
    }
}


import java.awt.*;
import javax.swing.*;
import java.awt.event.*;

public class JLis extends JFrame
{
    JLis()
    {
        getContentPane().setLayout(new FlowLayout());
        String str[]={"one","two","three","four","five"};
        JList li = new JList();
        li.setBackground(Color.red);
        li.setListData(str);
        int mode = ListSelectionModel.SINGLE_INTERVAL_SELECTION;
        li.setSelectionMode(mode);
        JScrollPane sc = new
        JScrollPane(li,JScrollPane.VERTICAL_SCROLLBAR_ALWAYS,JScrollPane.
        HORIZONTAL_SCROLLBAR_AS_NEEDED);
      getContentPane().add(sc);
    }
    public static void main(String argfs[])
    {
        JLis ls = new JLis();
        ls.setVisible(true);
        ls.setSize(300,300);
        //System.out.println(ListSelectionModel.MULTIPLE_INTERVAL_SELECTION);
    }
}


import java.awt.*;
import java.awt.event.*;
```

```
import javax.swing.*;
/*
<applet code="JRadioButtonDemo" width=300 height=200>
</applet>
*/

public class JRadioButtonDemo extends JApplet implements ActionListener
{
    TextArea tf;

    public void init()
    {
        Container contentPane= getContentPane();
        contentPane.setLayout(new FlowLayout());

        JRadioButton b1 = new JRadioButton("A");
        b1.addActionListener(this);
        contentPane.add(b1);

        JRadioButton b2 = new JRadioButton("B");
        b2.addActionListener(this);
        contentPane.add(b2);

        JRadioButton b3 = new JRadioButton("C");
        b3.addActionListener(this);
        contentPane.add(b3);

        ButtonGroup bg = new ButtonGroup();
        bg.add(b1);
        bg.add(b2);
        bg.add(b3);

        tf = new TextArea(1,0);
        contentPane.add(tf);
    }

    public void actionPerformed(ActionEvent ae)
    {
        tf.append(ae.getActionCommand());
    }
}
```

To run the above program without browser the syntax is
>appletviewer filename.java

```
import java.awt.*;
import javax.swing.*;
import java.awt.event.*;

public class colo extends JFrame implements ActionListener
{
    JColorChooser jc;
    //JFileChooser jc;
    JPanel pp;
    JButton btn;
    colo()
    {
        getContentPane().setLayout(new FlowLayout());
        pp=new JPanel();
        btn = new JButton("Select");
        getContentPane().add(btn);
        jc = new JColorChooser();
        getContentPane().add(jc);
        btn.addActionListener(this);
        pp.setBackground(Color.green);
        pp.setSize(150,150);
        getContentPane().add(pp);
    }
    public static void main(String ags[])
    {
        colo cc = new colo();
        cc.setVisible(true);
        cc.setSize(300,200);
    }
    public void actionPerformed(ActionEvent ae)
    {
    System.out.println("ckkk");
    pp.setBackground(jc.getColor());
    }
}
```

```
import javax.swing.*;
import java.awt.*;
import java.awt.event.*;

//<applet code = swg4 width=300 height=200></applet>
public class swg4 extends JApplet implements ItemListener
{
    public void init()
    {
        getContentPane().setLayout(new FlowLayout());
        JComboBox cb1 = new JComboBox();
```

```
        cb1.addItem("aaa");
        cb1.addItem("bbb");
        cb1.addItem("ccc");
        getContentPane().add(cb1);
        cb1.addItemListener(this);
    }
    public void itemStateChanged(ItemEvent ei)
    {
        if(ei.getStateChange()==ItemEvent.SELECTED)
        {
            System.out.println((String)(ei.getItem())+"was selected");
            showStatus((String)(ei.getItem())+"was selected");
        }
    }
}
```

```
import javax.swing.*;
import java.awt.*;
import javax.swing.border.*;

class Tab extends JFrame
{
    public Tab ()
    {
        JTabbedPane Jt = new JTabbedPane ();
        JPanel JP1 = new JPanel ();
        JPanel JP2 = new JPanel ();
        JP1.setBackground(Color.red);
        JP2.setBackground(Color.yellow);

        JButton btn1 = new JButton("First");
        JButton btn2 = new JButton("Second");

        JP1.add(btn1);
        JP2.add(btn2);

        Jt.addTab ("First", JP1);
        Jt.addTab ("Second", JP2);

        Jt.setSelectedIndex(0);
        getContentPane ().setLayout (new BorderLayout ());
        getContentPane ().add(Jt, BorderLayout.CENTER);

        JP1.setBorder(new TitledBorder("panel..1"));
        btn2.setBorder(new TitledBorder("btn2"));
    }
```

```
    public static void main (String ar[])
    {
        Tab t =new Tab ();
        t.setVisible (true);
        t.setTitle ("Tabbed Pane");
        t.setSize (400,300);
    }
}
```

```
import java.awt.*;
import java.awt.event.*;
import javax.swing.*;

/*<applet code = progress width=300 height=200>
</applet>*/

public class progress extends JApplet implements Runnable
{
    ProgressMonitor monitor;
    JFrame frame;
    public void init()
    {
        frame = new JFrame();
        int min =0;
        int max = 100;
        String[] message = new String[2];
        message[0] = ("Performing Operation ..");
        message[1] = ("This may take some time ...");
        monitor = new ProgressMonitor(frame,message,"Iteration",min,max);
    }
    public void run()
    {
        for(int i = 1; i <= 100; i++)
        {
            try{
                monitor.setNote("Iteration : "+i+"%");
                monitor.setProgress(i);
                if(monitor.isCanceled())
                {
                    monitor.setProgress(100);
                    break;
                }
                Thread.sleep(500);
            }catch(InterruptedException e){ }
        }
        monitor.close();
    }
```

```
    public void start()
    {
       Thread th = new Thread(this);
       th.start();
    }
}
```

```
import javax.swing.*;
import java.awt.*;
import java.awt.event.*;

public class JTf extends JFrame implements ActionListener
{
    JTextArea ta2;
    JTextField tf;
    JTf()
    {
       getContentPane().setLayout(new FlowLayout());
       JLabel lb = new JLabel("Name",new ImageIcon("Ms.gif"),JLabel.CENTER);
       tf = new JTextField(10);
       JTextArea ta1 = new JTextArea(10,10);
       ta1.setFont(new Font("TimesRoman",Font.BOLD,10));
       ta1.setForeground(Color.red);
       ta1.setBackground(Color.green);
       ta2 = new JTextArea(10,10);
       JScrollPane sc = new
       JScrollPane(ta2,JScrollPane.VERTICAL_SCROLLBAR_ALWAYS,JScrollPane.
       HORIZONTAL_SCROLLBAR_AS_NEEDED);
       getContentPane().add(lb);
       getContentPane().add(tf);
       getContentPane().add(ta1);
       getContentPane().add(sc);
       tf.addActionListener(this);
    }
    public static void main(String atgs[])
    {
       JTf jt = new JTf();
       jt.setVisible(true);
       jt.setSize(300,300);
    }
    public void actionPerformed(ActionEvent ae)
    {
       ta2.append(tf.getText()+"\n");
    }
}
```

```
import java.awt.*;
import java.awt.event.*;
import javax.swing.*;
/*
<applet code="JCheckBoxDemo" width =400 height=100>
</applet>
*/

public class JCheckBoxDemo extends JApplet implements ItemListener
{
   JTextField jtf;

   public void init() {

      Container contentPane = getContentPane();
      contentPane.setLayout(new FlowLayout());

      JCheckBox cb = new JCheckBox("C");
      cb.addItemListener(this);
      contentPane.add(cb);

      cb = new JCheckBox("C++");
      cb.addItemListener(this);
      contentPane.add(cb);

      cb = new JCheckBox("Java");
      cb.addItemListener(this);
      contentPane.add(cb);

      cb = new JCheckBox("Perl");
      cb.addItemListener(this);
      contentPane.add(cb);

      jtf = new JTextField(15);
      contentPane.add(jtf);
   }

   public void itemStateChanged(ItemEvent ie)
   {
      JCheckBox cb = (JCheckBox) ie.getItem();
      jtf.setText(cb.getText());
   }
}
```

❑❑❑

Chapter **13** *Networking*

INTRODUCTION

A network is a set of computers and peripherals, which are physically connected together. Networking enables sharing of resources and communication. Internet is a network of networks. Networking in java is possible through the use of java.net package.

Protocols assigning set of rules for communication between computers and between the networks. Java networking is done using TCP/IP and UDP protocols.

Client/Server

A computer which requests for some service from another computer is known as client.

The one that processes the request is called as server.

IP Address

Every computer connected to a network has a unique IP address. IP address is a 32-bit number which has four numbers separated by periods.

Ex. of IP address is

80.0.0.53

Port Number

Port number is assigned to all protocols, 21 are assigned for FTP, 23 are assigned for Telnet, etc.

TYPES OF NETWORKING PROGRAMS

There are two types of networking program they are :

- Connection oriented protocols is TCP/IP (Transmission control protocols)
- Connectionless protocols are UDP (User datagram protocols).

The supporting package is java.net.*;

Classes of java.net Package

Datagram, DatagramPacket, DatagramSocket are classes of java.net package for connectionless protocols.

Socket, ServerSocket is classes of java.net package for connection oriented protocols.

Implementation of Networking Programs

1. Compile the both client and server program.
2. Run the server program in one machine
3. Run the client in another machine
4. If you want do the same in same machines you have open two DOS-prompt, one for client and another one server.

Examples for both type are as follows :

```
import java.net.*;
class inetaddresstest
{
    public static void main(String args[])throws Exception
    {
        try
        {
            InetAddress add=InetAddress.getLocalHost();
            System.out.println("the address of the local host is...."+ add);
        }
        catch(Exception u)
        {
            System.out.println(u);
        }
    }
}


import java.net.*;
import java.io.*;

class datagramserver
{
    static DatagramSocket ds;
    static int cport=9,sport=8;
    public static void main(String args[])throws Exception
    {
        byte ff[]=new byte[1024];
        ds=new DatagramSocket(sport);
        BufferedReader dis=new BufferedReader(new InputStreamReader(System.in));
        System.out.println("server is waiting for input");
```

```
        //InetAddress ia=InetAddress.getLocalHost();
        InetAddress ia=InetAddress.getByName("80.0.1.16");

        while(true)
        {
            String str=dis.readLine();
            if((str==null||str.equals("end")))
            break;
            ff=str.getBytes();
            ds.send(new DatagramPacket(ff,str.length(),ia,cport));
        }
    }
}
```

```
import java.net.*;
import java.io.*;
class datagramclient
{
    static DatagramSocket ds;
    static byte ff[]=new byte[1024];
    static int cport=9,sport=8;
    public static void main(String args[])throws Exception
    {
        ds=new DatagramSocket(cport);
        System.out.println("client is waiting for server to send the data");
        System.out.println("press control c to come to the dos prompt");
        while(true)
        {
            DatagramPacket p=new DatagramPacket(ff,ff.length);
            ds.receive(p);
            String psx=new String(p.getData(),0,p.getLength());
            System.out.println(psx);
        }
    }
}
```

```
import java.net.*;

class Client
{
    public static void main (String ads[]) throws Exception
    {
        byte buf[] = new byte[1024];
```

```
        DatagramSocket Ds = new DatagramSocket (170);

        while (true)
        {
            DatagramPacket Dp= new DatagramPacket (buf, 1024);
            Ds.receive (Dp);
            String a = new String (Dp.getData(), 0, Dp.getLength());
            System.out.println (a);
        }
    }
}
```

```
import java.net.*;
import java.io.*;
class Server
{
    public static void main (String as[]) throws Exception
    {

        DatagramSocket Ds = new DatagramSocket (180);
        BufferedReader Bf = new BufferedReader (new InputStreamReader
                                                        (System.in));

        while (true)
        {
            String s = Bf.readLine ();
            if((s==null)||(s.equals("end")))
            break;
            Ds.send (new DatagramPacket
            (s.getBytes(),s.length(),InetAddress.getLocalHost(),170));
        }
    }
}
```

```
import java.net.*;
import java.io.*;
public class TServer
{
    public static void main(String args[]) throws Exception
    {
        ServerSocket ss=new ServerSocket(95);
        // ServerSocket s2 = new ServerSocket(int port,int maxque);
        Socket cs=ss.accept();
```

```
        System.out.println("connected to"+cs);
        PrintWriter out=new PrintWriter(cs.getOutputStream(),true);
        String inputline,outputline;
        BufferedReader stdin=new BufferedReader(new
                                         InputStreamReader(System.in));
        System.out.println("enter data in server");
        String s=stdin.readLine();
        File f=new File(s);
        if(f.exists())
        {
            BufferedReader d=new BufferedReader(new FileReader(s));
            String line;
            while((line=d.readLine())!=null)
            {
                out.write(line);
                out.flush();
            }
            d.close();
        }
        out.close();
        cs.close();
        ss.close();
    }
}
```

```
import java.net.*;
import java.io.*;
public class TClient
{
    public static void main(String args[]) throws Exception
    {
        Socket echoSocket=new Socket(args[0],95);//InetAddress.getLocalHost(),95);
        BufferedReader in=new BufferedReader(new
        InputStreamReader(echoSocket.getInputStream()));
        String userInput;
        while((userInput=in.readLine())!=null)
        System.out.println(userInput);
        in.close();
        echoSocket.close();
    }
}
```

```
import java.awt.*;
import java.awt.event.*;
```

```
import java.net.*;
import java.applet.*;
//<applet code=ur width=300 height=200></applet>
public class ur extends Applet implements ActionListener
{
    Button btn;
    public void init()
    {
        btn = new Button("click");
        setLayout(new FlowLayout());
        btn.addActionListener(this);
        add(btn);
    }
    public void actionPerformed(ActionEvent ae)
    {
        try
        {
            URL uu = new URL("http ://hotmail.com/");
            URLConnection uc = uu.openConnection();
            showStatus("the"+uc);
        }catch(Exception e){}
    }
}
```

❑❑❑

Chapter 14 Threads

DEFINITION

The thread is similar to a program that has a single flow of control.

The program that contains multiple flows of control is known as multithreaded programming.

Supporting Package

The thread supporting classes are resides in the java.lang.* package.

Two Way of Thread Programming

We can develop thread based application in two ways *i.e.,* is either by using inbuilt Thread class or Runnable interface. There is no difference between this two types but it is based on the user requirements.

If we are using Thread class it executes its own run () method or if we are using the interface Runnable it executes the run method of some other objects.

Example with Thread class :

```
Public class CounterThread extends Thread
{
   public void run()
   {
      for (int i=1;i<=10;i++)
      System.out.println("Counting " +i);
   }
   public static void main(String args[])
   {
      CounterThread ct = new CounterThread();
      ct.start();
   }
}
```

In this program the start( ) method indirectly calls the run( ) method.

Example with Runnable Interface :

```
Public class RunCounter implements Runnable
{
    public void run()
    {
        for(int i=10;i>=10;i–)
        System.out.println("Counting down" + i);
    }

    public static void main(String args[])
    {
        Runcounter rc = new Runcounter();
        Thread td = new Thread(rc);
        td.start();
    }
}
```

LIFE CYCLE OF THREAD

1. New born state
2. Runnable state
3. Running state
4. Blocked state
5. Dead State.

New Born State

When we create a thread object, the thread is said to be new born state. In this state we can apply to methods either start( ) or stop( ).

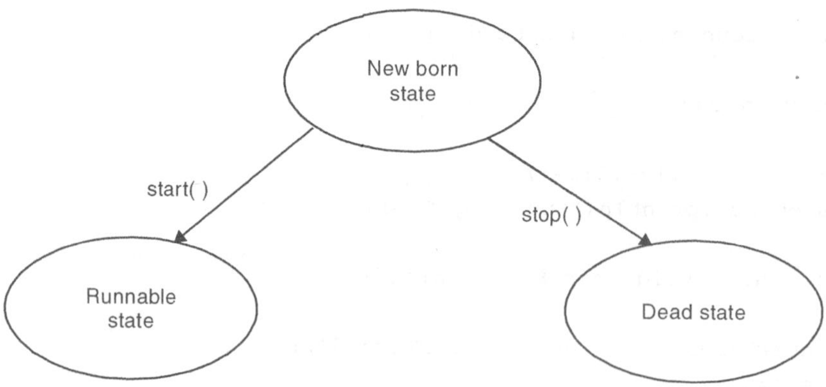

Figure 14.1

Runnable State

The runnable state means that the thread is ready for execution and is waiting for the availability of the processor. If more than one thread waiting for execution actually it will work first come first service manner. In this state, the yield( ) method is used to cause the currently running threads into ready state (runnable state).

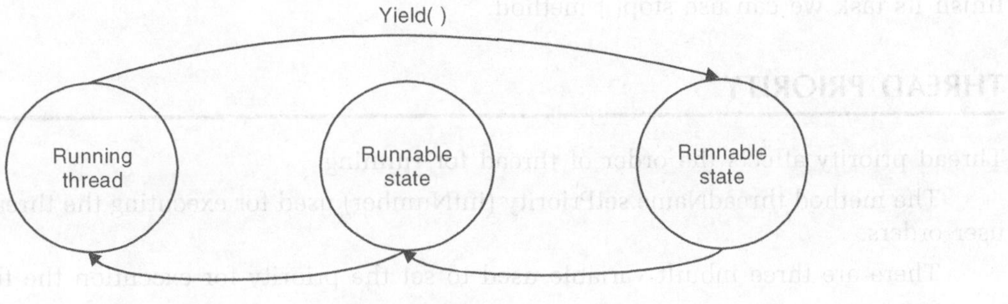

Figure 14.2

Running State

In this state the processor assigns time to the thread for its execution.

In this stage, the following methods are applied to the running state thread.

Blocked State

1. Suppose we want to suspend a thread for some time, we can apply suspend( ) and to wakeup the thread use resume( ) method.

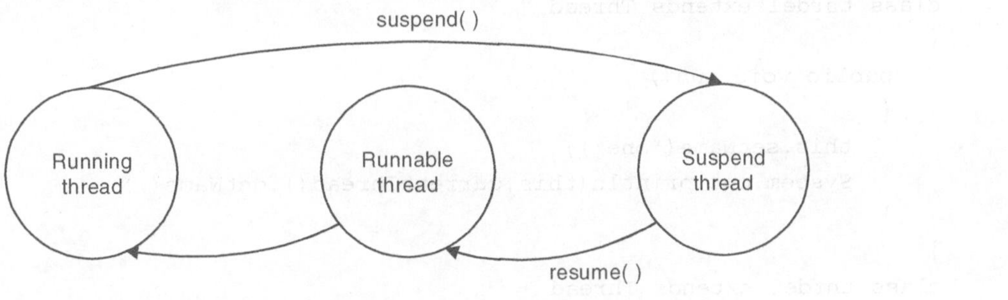

Figure 14.3

2. Suppose we want to make the thread to sleep for some time, use sleep( ) method. After the time is elapsed that will enter into runnable stage.

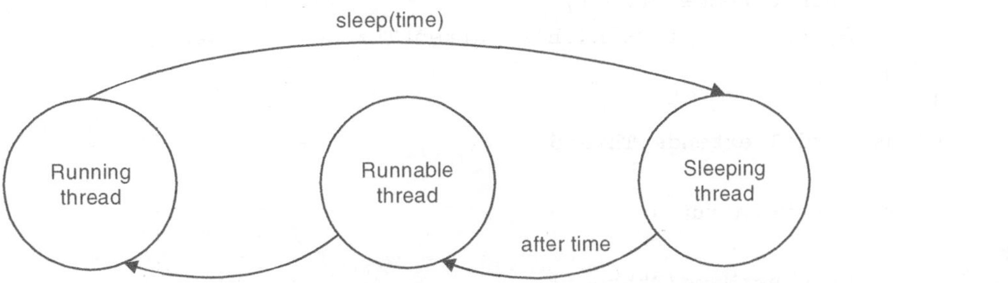

Figure 14.4

3. To make the thread to wait until some event occurs use wait( ) method, then this will wakeup by using notify( ) method.

Dead State

Once the thread finishes its running stage enters naturally into dead stage. If we want force to finish its task we can use stop( ) method.

THREAD PRIORITY

Thread priority affects the order of thread for running.

The method threadName.setPriority (intNumber) used for executing the threads as per the user orders.

There are three inbuilt variable used to set the priority for execution the thread

MIN_PRIORITY	=	1	
NORM_PRIORITY	=	5	DEFAULT
MAX_PRIORITY	=	10	

Synchronization

Two or more thread access the same data leads to loss of data. To avoid this data's are placed inside the synchronized block leads to accessing data in sequence manner.

Examples :

```
class thrde1 extends Thread
{
    public void run()
    {
        this.setName("one");
        System.out.println(this.currentThread().getName());
    }
}
class thrde2 extends Thread
{
    public void run()
    {
        this.setName("two");
        System.out.println(this.currentThread().getName());
    }
}
class thrde3 extends Thread
{
    public void run()
    {
        this.setName("three");
        System.out.println(this.currentThread().getName());
    }
```

```
    public static void main(String aet[])
    {
       thrde1 td1 = new thrde1();
       thrde2 td2 = new thrde2();
       thrde3 td3 = new thrde3();

       td1.start();
       td2.start();
       td3.start();

       td1.setPriority(Thread.MAX_PRIORITY);
       td3.setPriority(5);
       td2.setPriority(1);
    }
}


class syn1 extends Thread
{
    public void run()
    {
       call.comm(this.currentThread().getName());
    }
}
class syn2 extends Thread
{
    public void run()
    {
       call.comm(this.currentThread().getName());
    }
}
class syn3 extends Thread
{
    public void run()
    {
       call.comm(this.currentThread().getName());
    }
}
class call
{
    static void comm(String str)
    {
       System.out.println(str);
       syn1 s1 = new syn1();
       syn2 s2 = new syn2();
```

```
        syn3 s3 = new syn3();

        s1.start();
        s3.start();
        s2.start();
        for(int i=0;i<10;i++)
        if(i==5)
        break;
    }
    public static void main(String args[])
    {
    comm("kabi");
    }
}


//<applet code = moving width=400 height=200></applet>

import java.awt.*;
import java.applet.Applet;

public class moving extends Applet implements Runnable
{
    Thread t=null;
    int p=0;
    int x=0;
    Image i1;
    Image i2;
    public void init()
    {
        i1=getImage(getCodeBase(),"juggler3.gif");
        // i2=getImage(getCodeBase(),"santa workshop.gif");
    }
    public void start()
    {
        t=new Thread(this);
        t.start();
    }
    public void run()
    {
        while(true)
        {
            for(p=0;p<getSize().width;p+=5)
            {
                for(x=0;x<getSize().height;x+=50)
```

```
            {
               repaint();
               try
               {
                  t.sleep(1000);
               }catch(InterruptedException i){};
            }
         }
      }
   }
   public void stop()
   {
      t.stop();
      t=null;
   }
   public void paint(Graphics h)
   {
      h.drawImage(i1,30+p,5+x,this);
      h.drawImage(i1,100+x,200+p,this);
   }
}
```

□□□

Chapter **15**

JDBC (Java Database Connectivity)

INTRODUCTION

JDBC APIs provides to develop the application with java front end and database with back end. The supporting package is java.sql.*. The database is Sybase, Informix, Ingress, MS-access, and oracle., sql we can use as the back end tool. The java.sql.* API provides set of classes and interfaces to enable programmers to write pure java database applications.

The following are the characteristics of JDBC:

1. It is a call – level SQL interface for java.
2. It does not restrict the type of queries passed to an underlying DBMS(database management system) driver.
3. JDBC mechanisms are simple to understand and use.
4. It provides a java interface that stays consistent with the rest of the java system.
5. JDBC may be implemented on top of common SQL level APIs.
6. It uses strong, static typing whenever possible.

Microsoft ODBC is not sufficient to connect to the database by java. To overcome the problem JDBC driver arises.

Some of the advantages of using java with JDBC are :

1. Easy and economical.
2. Continued usage of already installed databases.
3. Development time is short.
4. Installation and version control simplified.

JDBC does the following three things:

1. Establish connection with a database.
2. Send sql statements.
3. Process the results

JDBC VS ODBC

The most widely used interface to acess relational database today is MS ODBC API. ODBC performs similar tasks as that of JDBC and yet JDBC is preferred due to the following reasons:

1. ODBC cannot be directly used with java because it uses a C interface.
2. ODBC makes use of pointers which have been totally removed from java.
3. ODBC is complex one when compared to it JDBC is easy.
4. ODBC is manual Installations but JDBC is automatically installed in all platforms.

Different Types of Driver Managers

There are four different types of JDBC drivers:

1. The JDBC-ODBC Bridge plus ODBC driver.
2. Native-API partly—java driver.
3. JDBC-Net pure java driver.
4. Native-protocol pure java driver.

Syntax for Connection

DriverManager.getConnection(String url(jdbc :odbc :dsn name), String user, String password);

url is jdbc :odbc :subname.

The subname is created as follows :

1. Click the control panel
2. Click the Administrative tools
3. Select the ODBC
4. Click the add button
5. Select the database driver
6. click the finish button
7. enter the dsn name
8. enter the password
9. select the database
10. click the ok button
11. this dsn, password name is given getConnection method

Steps for using JDBC

There are seven basic steps for using JDBC to access a database. They are :

1. Import the java.sql package
2. Register the driver
3. Connect to the database
4. Create a statement
5. Execute the statement
6. Retrieve the results
7. Close the statement and the connection

Examples :

```
import java.sql.*;
public class jdbc1
{
   public static void main(String args[])
   {
      try
      {
         Class.forName("sun.jdbc.odbc.JdbcOdbcDriver");
         Connection conn=DriverManager.getConnection("jdbc:odbc:kabi",
                                                     "scott","tiger");
         Statement stnt=conn.createStatement();
         int x = stnt.executeUpdate("update kab set age=10 where age=200");
         System.out.println("rowsupdated");
      }catch (Exception e)
      {
         System.out.println (" Error :" + e);
      }
   }
}
```

```
import java.sql.*;
class jdbc2
{
   public static void main(String args[])throws SQLException,
                                              ClassNotFoundException
   {
      Class.forName("sun.jdbc.odbc.JdbcOdbcDriver");
      try
      {
         Connection conn=DriverManager.getConnection("jdbc :odbc :sanjay",
                                                     "dummy","ssi");
         Statement stnt=conn.createStatement();
         ResultSet rs=stnt.executeQuery("select * from tz2");
         while(rs.next())
         {
            System.out.println(rs.getInt(1));
            System.out.println(rs.getString(2));
         }

         rs.close();
         stnt.close();
```

```
            conn.close();
        }catch(Exception ex){}
    }
}

import java.sql.*;
class jdbc3
{
    public static void main(String args[])throws SQLException,
                                                  ClassNotFoundException
    {
        Class.forName("sun.jdbc.odbc.JdbcOdbcDriver");
        Connection conn=DriverManager.getConnection("jdbc :odbc :sanjay",
                                                        "dummy","ssi");
        System.out.println("connected successfully to the database");
        System.out.println("creating table master_details3");
        Statement stnt=conn.createStatement();
        String sqlstring="create table master_details1(shareid number(3),compname
        varchar2(20),noofshares number(4),purrate number(6,2),purdate
        date,currrate number(6,2))";
        String sqlstring1="create table details111(shareid number(3),certno
        varchar2(10),noofshares number(3),firstholder varchar2(15),secondholder
        varchar2(15))";

        stnt.execute(sqlstring);
        stnt.execute(sqlstring1);
        System.out.println("table created master_details3");
        System.out.println("table created _details11");

        /* sqlstring="select * from master_details33";
        sqlstring="select * from details11";
        ResultSet rs=stnt.executeQuery(sqlstring);
        if(rs!=null)
        {
            while(rs.next())
            {
                System.out.println(rs.getString(1));
                System.out.println(rs.getString(2));
            }
        } */
    }
}


import java.sql.*;
import java.io.*;
import java.lang.String;
class jdbc4
{
```

```
    public static void main(String args[]) throws Exception
    {
       Class.forName("sun.jdbc.odbc.JdbcOdbcDriver");
       Connection conn=DriverManager.getConnection("jdbc:odbc:sanjay",
                                                   "dummy","ssi");
       System.out.println("connected successfully to the database");
       System.out.println("Do you want to continue ?");
       Statement stnt=conn.createStatement();
       try
       {
          char resp='y';

          while((char) System.in.read()=='y')
          {
             BufferedReader b=new BufferedReader(new InputStreamReader(System.in));
             String chk=b.readLine();
             String str=readEntry("enter the insert statement");

             stnt.executeUpdate(str);
             System.out.println("one row inserted");
             System.out.println("Do you want to insert another row(y/n) ?");
          }
       }catch(SQLException ex){
          System.out.println("the SQL Exception raised is"+ex);
       }
       stnt.close();
       conn.close();
    }
    static String readEntry(String prompt)
    {
       try
       {
          StringBuffer buffer=new StringBuffer();
          System.out.print(prompt);
          System.out.flush();
          BufferedReader br=new BufferedReader(new InputStreamReader(System.in));
          String c=br.readLine();
          return c;
       }catch(IOException e)
       {
          return"e";
       }
    }
}

import java.sql.*;
class customer
{
    public static void main(String args[])throws SQLException,ClassNotFoundException
```

```
    {
        Class.forName("sun.jdbc.odbc.JdbcOdbcDriver");
        Connection conn= DriverManager.getConnection("jdbc:odbc:sanjay",
                                                     "dummy","ssi");
        System.out.println("connected successfully to the database");
        try
        {
            Statement stnt=conn.createStatement();
            ResultSet rs=stnt.executeQuery("select 'connected' from dual");
            rs.next();
            String s=rs.getString(1);
            System.out.println(s);
            stnt.close();
            conn.close();
        }catch(Exception ex){
            System.out.println("the exception raised is"+ex);
        }
    }
}

import java.sql.*;
class jdbc6
{
    public static void main(String args[])throws Exception
    {
        Class.forName("sun.jdbc.odbc.JdbcOdbcDriver");
        Connection conn=DriverManager.getConnection("jdbc:odbc :madhuri",
                                                    "dummy","ssi");
        try{
            System.out.println("connected successfully to the database");
            System.out.println("altering table detailsl1");
            Statement stnt=conn.createStatement();
            stnt.executeUpdate("alter table tel modify(address varchar2(70))");
            System.out.println("table tel altered");
        }catch (Exception er){
            System.out.println("the exception is raised"+er);
        }
    }
}

import java.sql.*;

public class jdbc
{
    public jdbc()
    {
        try
        {
```

```
            String dn = "sun.jdbc.odbc.JdbcOdbcDriver";
            Driver dd = (Driver)Class.forName(dn).newInstance();
            String dburl = "jdbc:odbc:student";
            if(dd.acceptsURL(dburl))
            {
               System.out.println("url is valid");
            }
            else
            {
               System.out.println("url is not valid");
            }
         }
         catch(Exception e){}
      }
      public static void main(String args[])
      {
         jdbc jd = new jdbc();
      }
   }
```

```
import java.sql.*;

public class drop
{
   public static void main(String arg[])
   {
      try
      {
         Class.forName("sun.jdbc.odbc.JdbcOdbcDriver");
         Connection c = DriverManager.getConnection("jdbc:odbc:g","dummy","ssi");
         Statement s = c.createStatement();
         s.execute("drop table ssi3");
         System.out.println("Table droped.......");

         s.close();
         c.close();
      }catch(Exception e)
      {
         System.out.println("Some error" +e);
      }
   }
}
```

❑❑❑

Chapter **16** **_The java.util.* package_**

BASICS OF UTIL PACKAGE

The java.util package provides 34 classes and 13 interfaces that support Collection API., date/ calendar operations, internationalization, parsing, and basic event processing. The package is used to work mainly with date and calendars.

The example of classes is GregorianCalendar, SimpleTimeZone and Timezone. The Date class is responsible for encapsulating date and time information. The StringTokenizer class provides methods to parse a string.

Examples :

```
Import java.lang.*; (default package)
Import java.util.*;

Public class StrToken
{
   public static void main(String args[])
   {
      StringTokenzier token = new StringTokenizer(" This is a test for tokens"):
      While(token.hasMoreTokens())
      {
         System.out.println(token.nextToken());
      }
   }
}
```

Output

this
is

a
test
for
tokens

```
//Example for Aloirthms class of java.util.*;

import java.util.*;

public class alog
{
   public static void main(String pp[]);
   {
      LinkedList l1 = new LinkedList();
      l1.add(new Integer(-8));
      l1.add(new Integer(20));
      l1.add(new Integer(-20));
      l1.add(new Integer(8));

      Comparator co = new Collections.reverseOrder();
      Collections.sort(l1,co);

      Iterator li = l1.iterator();
      System.out.println("List sorted in reverse :");
      while(li.hasNext())
      System.out.print(li.next() + "");
      System.out.println();

      Collections.shuffle(l1);
      li = l1.iterator();
      System.out.println("List shuffled :");
      while(li.hasNext())
      System.out.print(li.next() + "");
      System.out.println();

      System.out.println("Minimum :" + Collections.min(l1));
      System.out.println("Maximum :" + Collections.max(l1));
   }
}


public class ru
{
   public static void main(String at[])throws Exception
```

```
    {
        Runtime rn = Runtime.getRuntime();
        rn.exec("c :/windows.000/notepad.exe");

        /*String s1 = new String("abc");
        String s2 = new String("ABC");
        System.out.println(s1.compareTo(s2));*/
    }
}

import java.util.*;

public class SetExample
{
    public static void main(String args[])
    {
        Set set = new HashSet();
        set.add("Bernadine");
        set.add("Elizabeth");
        set.add("Gene");
        set.add("Elizabeth");
        set.add("Clara");
        System.out.println(set);//no duplicates
        Set sortedSet = new TreeSet(set);
        System.out.println(sortedSet);//sorted
    }
}
/*[Gene, Clara, Bernadine, Elizabeth]
[Bernadine, Clara, Elizabeth, Gene]
*/

//Example for Hashtable class of java.util.*;

import java.util.*;

public class hashtdemo
{
    public static void main(String pp[])
    {
        Hashtable hs = new Hashtable();
        Enumeration enu;
        String str;
        double bal;
```

```
        hs.put("John",new Double(3456.2));
        hs.put("Sara",new Double(6734.232));
        hs.put("Naren",new Double(6876.122));
        hs.put("Nithya",new Double(3344.56));
        hs.put("Sasi",new Double(539.84));

        enu = hs.keys();
        while (enu.hasMoreElements())
        {
            str = (String)enu.nextElement();
            System.out.println(str + " :" + hs.get(str));
        }
        System.out.println();

        bal = ((Double)hs.get("Sara")).doubleValue();
        hs.put("Sara",new Double(bal+1000));
        System.out.println("Sara's new balance :" + hs.get("Sara"));
    }
}


//Example for vector class of java.util*;

import java.util.*;

class vectordemo
{
    public static void main(String pp[])
    {
        Vector ve = new Vector(3,2);

        System.out.println("Initial size : "+ ve.size());
        System.out.println("Initial capacity :" + ve.capacity());
        ve.addElement(new Integer(1));
        ve.addElement(new Integer(2));
        ve.addElement(new Integer(3));
        ve.addElement(new Integer(4));
        System.out.println("Capacity after 4 additions :" + ve.capacity());

        ve.addElement(new Double(5.451));
        System.out.println("Current capacity :" + ve.capacity());

        ve.addElement(new Double(6.081));
        ve.addElement(new Integer(7));
        System.out.println("Current capacity :" + ve.capacity());
```

```
    ve.addElement(new Float(9.41));
    ve.addElement(new Integer(19));
    System.out.println("Current capacity :" + ve.capacity());

    ve.addElement(new Integer(10));
    ve.addElement(new Integer(11));
    System.out.println("First element :" + (Integer)ve.firstElement());
    System.out.println("Last element :" + (Integer)ve.lastElement());

    if(ve.contains(new Integer(30)))
    System.out.println("Vector contains 3");

    Enumeration enu = ve.elements();
    System.out.println("\n Elements in Vector :");
    while(enu.hasMoreElements())
    System.out.print(enu.nextElement() +" ");
    System.out.println();

    /* Iterator ite = ve.iterator();
    System.out.println("\n Elements in Vector :");
    while(ite.hasNext())
    System.out.print(ite.next() +" ");
    System.out.println(); */
  }
}
```

❑❑❑

Index

❑❑❑